THE
WHITE
RAM

A
Story of

Abraham
and Isaac

MORDICAI GERSTEIN

Holiday House / *New York*

This book is dedicated to all our fellow animals,
from whom we take and receive so much

AUTHOR'S NOTE

In the Old Testament story of Abraham and his son, which is known to Jews,
Christians, and Muslims, a ram plays a small but essential role.
This is the story of that ram, based on Jewish legends called Midrashim,
which are tales about the stories of the Old Testament.
In the illustrations, following the Jewish tradition that
God may not be pictured, I used the empty spaces between clouds
to suggest images of His hands, and even His face.
See if you can find them.

Library of Congress Cataloging-in-Publication Data
Gerstein, Mordicai
The white ram : a story of Abraham and Isaac / Mordicai Gerstein.
p. cm.
Summary: A white ram, made on the sixth day of creation,
waits patiently in the garden of Eden until the time is right,
then runs to save a certain child in fulfillment
of God's plan.
ISBN-10: 0-8234-1897-9
ISBN-13: 978-0-8234-1897-8
[1. Rams—Fiction. 2. Rosh ha-Shanah—Fiction.
3. Fasts and feasts—Judaism—Fiction.
4. Abraham (Biblical patriarch)—Fiction.]
I. Title.
PZ7.G325Wh 2006
[E]—dc22
2005046001

Legend tells us
that on the last day
of the Creation, in the twilight
of the first Sabbath,
God made a white ram.

He put the ram in the garden of Eden
and said,
"Wait here until I call you."

And there the ram waited.

Adam and Eve,
the first man and first woman,
disobeyed God and had to leave Eden.
They became parents and farmers.
But the ram stayed and waited.

The ages passed. Other creatures left the garden.

Stars were born and stars died. Still the ram waited.

He waited till the morning
God woke him and said,
"Today is the day."
And the ram jumped up
and began to run.
He knew what he had to do.

The evil one appeared and said,
"Stop! Don't leave this beautiful garden.
It will mean your death!"

But the ram said,
"I must save the child!"
And he ran out of Eden.
He ran over hills of rocks and boulders.
He knew where he was going.

And the evil one appeared disguised as a field of green grass.
"Stop here!" he said. "Eat and rest.
There's no need to hurry."

But the ram replied, "I must save the child!"
And he ran faster.
He ran on and on over dry and dusty deserts.

And
the evil one
appeared
disguised
as a cool,
sparkling
fountain
and sang,
"Stop, drink
deep of me,
and rest.
There's no hurry."

"I can't stop!" cried the ram.
"I must save the child!"
And on he ran. He ran through dark swamps
and tangled jungles.

And the evil one appeared disguised
as a fierce lion and roared,
"Stop! Or I'll tear you to pieces and devour you!"

But the ram replied, "I must save the child!"
And he leapt over the lion and ran on.

The ram ran till he came to the sacred mountain.
At the top he saw a child tied and
bound on an altar, and a weeping man.
"Wait!" cried the ram, running faster. "I am here! Take *me*!"

But the evil one, disguised as a bush of brambles,
caught the ram's horns and said,
"You shall go no farther!"
The ram struggled and cried, "Abraham! I am here! Take *me*!"
But the man, Abraham,
did not hear.

Then the ram heard the voice of God say to Abraham,
"Stop! I asked you to sacrifice your only son, Isaac,
to test your love and trust in me. Now, instead of Isaac, sacrifice this ram.
I made him in the twilight of the last day of the Creation for this moment,
to take Isaac's place on this altar."
And Abraham heard the voice of God, and untied Isaac,
who jumped up joyfully.

"But Lord," said Abraham.
"Why did you have to test me?
You know all things.
You *knew* that I would do
anything you asked,
even give you my only son."

"I knew," said the Lord.
"But I wanted the whole world
to see your love and your trust in me,
so that all people
might follow your example."
And Abraham said,
"Lord, in times to come, remember my love
and forgive the sins of Isaac,
and his children,
and his children's
children's children."

Abraham freed the ram from the brambles,
and the ram leapt onto the altar.

"Abraham," said the ram.
"On New Year's Day, Rosh Hashanah, blow through one of my horns,
and God will hear the sound and remember Isaac and me,
the white ram that took his place. And He will forgive the sins of Isaac,
and his children, and his children's children's children,
always, till the end of time."

Then the ram lay down on the altar,
and his soul flew into God's hands.

And from the ram's ashes
the mortar for the
altar of the great Temple
was made.

And from his bones,
on that mountain
the foundations
of Jerusalem were made.

And from his bowels
the ten strings
of King David's
harp were made.

And from
his hide the prophet
Elijah made
a cape.

And from his horns were made two shofars.
One was blown when Moses received
the Ten Commandments.

And the other will call the children
of Israel home.

And now, when the sound of the ram's horn
is heard on Rosh Hashanah,
we remember Isaac and Abraham.

And we remember the white ram
that now and forever
grazes in the fields of heaven.